APR 19 '90

APR 30 1993　　MAR 18 2000
MAY 21 1994　　MAY 10 2000
　MAR 27 1995　MAY 21 2000
DEC 19 1995
　FEB 27 1996　　DEC 26 2002
　MAY 14 1996
　　JUN 10 1996

　　JUL -3 1996
　FEB 27 1997
MAY -5 1998

APR 24 1997
DEC 7 1997

San Mateo Public Library
San Mateo, CA 94402-1592
Questions Answered

4 CONTENTS

WHAT ARE THEY?
6

WHERE THEY COME FROM
8

HOW THEY ARE MADE
10

SMUGGLERS
12

WHY PEOPLE USE THEM
14

WHAT IS THE EFFECT?
16

ADDICTION
22

SOCIETY SUFFERS
24

THE LAW
30

GLOSSARY
31

INDEX
32

Facts on
The Crack
and
Cocaine Epidemic

Clint Twist

FRANKLIN WATTS
New York · London · Toronto · Sydney

Design: David West
 Children's Book Design
Editor: Roger Vlitos
Editorial planning: Clark Robinson Ltd
Researcher: Cecilia Weston-Baker
Illustrator: Peter Harper
Photographic Credits:
Cover and pages 7t, 9t, 11t, 21t and m, 24, 25 all, 27b, 29b and 30b: Frank Spooner Agency; pages 4, 7b and 1, 11b, 17, 23t, 28 and 29t: David Browne; pages 8, 15b, 26r and 30t: Rex Features; page 9b: Popperfoto/Reuters; pages 10-11 and 19: Meiselas/Magnum; pages 12 and 23b: Vanessa Bailey; page 13: Abbas/Magnum; page 14: Goldwater/Network; page 15t: Griffiths/Magnum; page 18: Richards/Magnum; page 20: Peress/Magnum; page 22: Reed/Magnum; page 261 Newsday; page 27t: Scianna/Magnum

© Aladdin Books Ltd 1989

The publishers wish to point out that most of the photographs used in this book have been posed by models or obtained from photographic agencies.

Created and designed by
Aladdin Books Ltd
70 Old Compton Street
London W1

*First published in the
United States by*
Franklin Watts
387 Park Avenue South
New York, NY 10016

All rights reserved

Printed in Belgium

The publishers wish to acknowledge the help of
all those involved in producing this book, and
to thank them for their assistance; especially
Mary Treacy of the Standing Conference on Drug
Abuse, who has acted as a specialist consultant.

Library of Congress Cataloging-in-Publication Data

Twist, Clint.
 Facts on the crack and cocaine epidemic/by Clint Twist
  p. cm.
 Includes index
 Summary: explains what crack and cocaine are, how they are grown, purified, and transported, why people take cocaine, its effects, and society's reaction to the increase in cocaine use.
  ISBN 0-631-10822-8
  1. Cocaine habit-Juvenile literature. 2. Cocaine-Health aspects-Juvenile literature. 3. Crack (Drug)-Health aspects-Juvenile literature. (1. Cocaine. 2. Crack (Drug) 3. Drug abuse).
   I. Title II. Title: The crack and cocaine epidemic.
RC568.C6T96 1989
362.29'8--dc20   89-8909
                                                                CIP
                                                                AC

INTRODUCTION

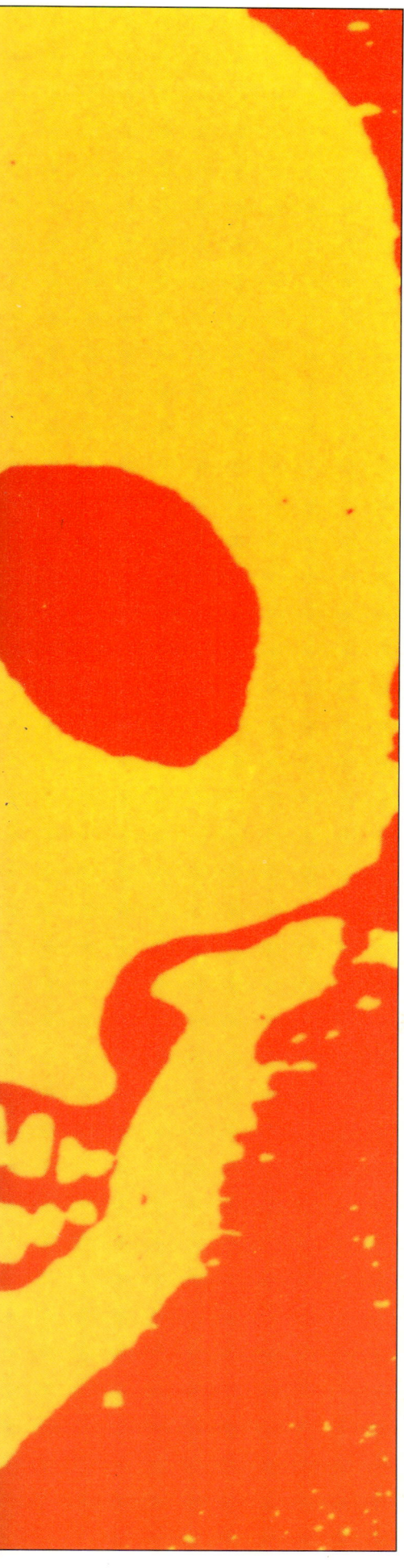

For many years, cocaine was the "champagne" drug of the rich and famous. Today it is taken by many different types of people, most of whom do not know how dangerous it can be. Both cocaine and crack can cause health problems and a reckless craving for the drugs. Crack users have become the No.1 drug problem in the United States. Crack has claimed many lives since it began to be sold on the streets only a few years ago. Its use has become an epidemic, spreading at an alarming rate, and bringing crime, death, destruction and misery with it. The message of the Crackdown campaign poster shown on the left says it all...
CRACK KILLS

6 WHAT ARE THEY?

Cocaine is a powerful drug, and like many others, its use is illegal without a doctor's guidance. However, there are very few cases in which this guidance is given. Even small amounts of cocaine can be dangerous to the brain and body. It is also very expensive, worth about six times its weight in gold. Crack is a form of cocaine that has been changed so that it can be smoked. Crack is usually sold in tiny quantities, so people think it is cheaper than cocaine. But crack is actually much more expensive and people soon develop a craving for it. Both of these drugs can cause awful personal problems and have harmful side-effects. People are often tempted to try them because of the short-term pleasure they give. But both of these dangerous drugs can cause pain, misery and death.

THE STREET SLANG
Cocaine has slang names like, "snow" or "dust," because of its white powdery appearance. Crack is often called "rocks" or "teeth" because of how it looks.

INNOCENT BEGINNINGS

Cocaine was first made about 100 years ago. Before people knew it could be dangerous, cocaine was widely used in dentistry and medicines. Even Coca Cola contained a small amount until 1903. By 1919, the use of cocaine, except under special licence, had been banned by international agreement.

Cocaine is a fine white powder. Doctors once used it as a painkiller and dentists gave it to their patients before pulling teeth out. It was also mixed in drinks and sold as a tonic in drug stores.

Crack is a recent invention. Drug pushers make more profit for themselves by selling crack instead of cocaine. Crack smokers quickly develop a craving for the drug, and come back again and again to buy it. Crack looks like tiny white pebbles. When it is heated it makes the cracking sound that gave it its name.

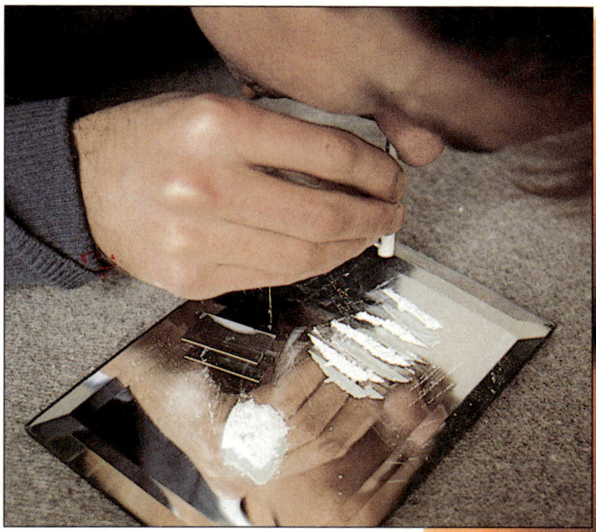

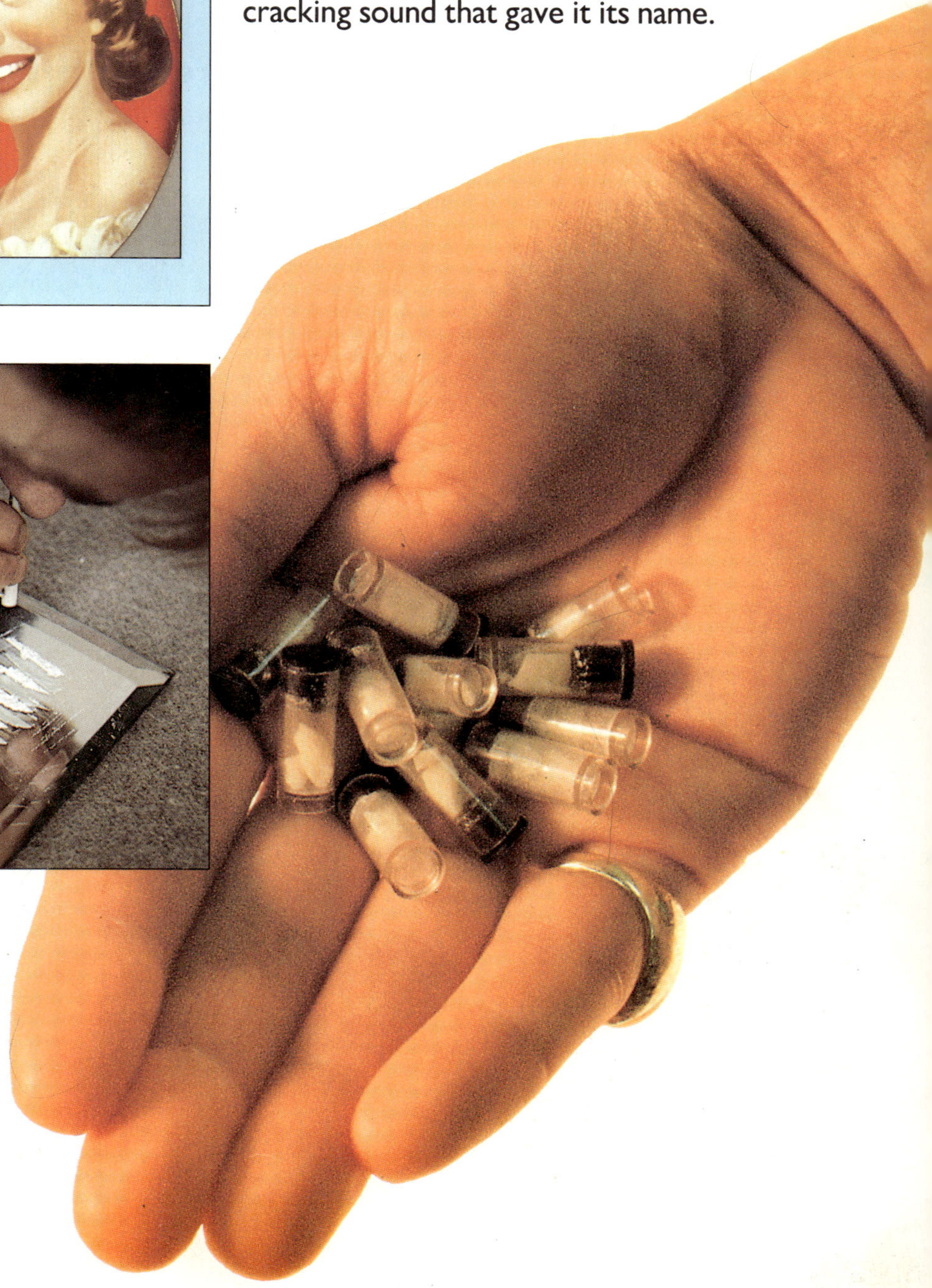

8 WHERE THEY COME FROM

Cocaine is processed from the leaves of the coca plant. This plant grows wild in the remote mountain regions of South America. The soil is fertile but the climate is only suitable for a few crops. Life was always very hard here. People have to climb up and down steep-sided valleys while breathing thin mountain air and get tired easily. Thousands of years ago, the Indians of these areas discovered that chewing coca leaves stopped them feeling tired or hungry. Many South American tribes still chew coca leaves while they work. Growing the plants, or chewing the leaves is not illegal. But cultivating them to convert the leaves into cocaine is against the law. Many poor farmers now grow coca secretly in order to get money from drug barons. Others are forced to do so.

THE DRUG BARONS

Billions of dollars worth of cocaine is sold every year. Most of it comes from a few rich and powerful people we call the "drug barons." They never touch cocaine themselves, but pay other people to break the law. They are clever and very difficult to catch. One of the most notorious, Carlos Lehder, was finally arrested in 1987. The drug barons have private armies who threaten and bribe for them. Their corruption often goes all the way to the top. Generals Meza and Noriega, the presidents of Bolivia and Panama, have been linked with drugs.

Lehder

Noriega

CASH-CROP COUNTRIES

The inhabitants of the South American mountains are poor peasants. Their usual crops, barley and maize, allow them to feed their families, but cannot be sold for much hard cash. Coca is an important crop for them because the drug barons give them a good cash price and pay for everything they can produce. As a result, coca is grown widely in Bolivia, Colombia, Ecuador and Peru.

SOUTH AMERICA

- Main cocaine producing countries
- Countries where coca plants grow

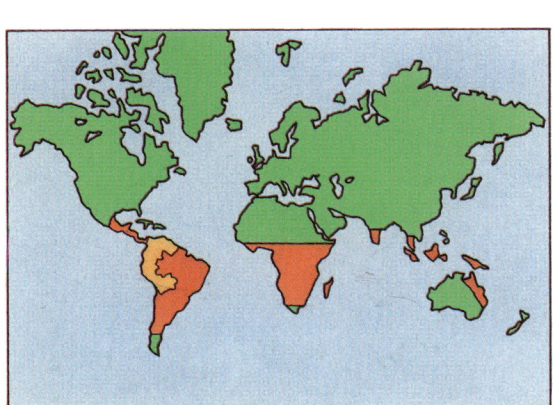

10 HOW THEY ARE MADE

Coca leaves only contain about 1 percent cocaine. Extracting the drug from the plant is a long and complicated process which involves a number of dangerous chemicals. The processing is carried out in secret jungle laboratories using crude equipment. Because of this, cocaine often contains poisonous impurities. The cocaine that is bought by the user on the street is never pure. A typical "deal" might contain only 20 percent cocaine. Drug dealers almost always mix cocaine with a cheap white powder in order to increase their profits. Sometimes this powder is fairly harmless – powdered milk is often used. But other addictive drugs, such as amphetamines or "speed," are often added. These can be even more dangerous than the cocaine itself.

HARVESTING

Coca grows fast, and can be harvested five or six times a year. An acre of land produces about 100 lbs of leaves. This yields about one pound of cocaine – in 1989 worth over $60,000.

After harvesting, the leaves are laid out in the sun to dry for a short while. They can then be chewed by the poor farmers or Indians, or converted into coca paste for sale to the drug barons who organize the cocaine processing.

PROCESSING THE PLANTS

The first stage of turning coca leaves into cocaine is to make coca paste. This is done by soaking the leaves in paraffin. As the leaves soften they are crushed into a paste. This is mixed with sulfuric acid (a powerful chemical that can easily dissolve metal), and then treated with hydrochloric acid (even more powerful). The result is a small amount of cocaine and a lot of dangerous waste chemicals.

MAKING "CRACK"

Crack is made by heating cocaine with baking soda. This process seldom produces the same result twice. A small amount of cocaine usually turns into crack, but there is a lot of leftover baking soda. The dealers don't care and waste nothing. They sell it all.

12 SMUGGLERS

Cocaine is illegal all over the world, except for a very few strictly-controlled medical uses. The only way the drug barons can transport cocaine is by smuggling it past the police and customs. Most smugglers are drug users or poor South Americans who are paid by the drug barons to take the risks. They could end up in jail or even dead. Small-scale smugglers are called "mules." They may be paid more money smuggling drugs than they could make in a lifetime of work on the right side of the law. Customs officials and police receive a thorough training: they know most of the tricks that these small-time smugglers use. But the drug barons don't mind if a few get caught. It keeps the officials busy while they sneak in even larger shipments elsewhere.

Cocaine is sometimes hidden inside imports like coffee, sugar, tires and timber. Smugglers often hide the drug in the lining of their clothes, or taped to their bodies in flat packets. Children's toys are a favorite hiding place. Customs officers have to suspect everybody, including children.

SMUGGLERS' TRICKS

Suitcases with false bottoms, hollowed-out statues and secret compartments in automobiles, are hiding places that are familiar to Customs officers. Some people try to smuggle cocaine inside their bodies by swallowing small packets of the drug wrapped in rubber or plastic. If one of these bursts inside the stomach the result is a sudden and painful death.

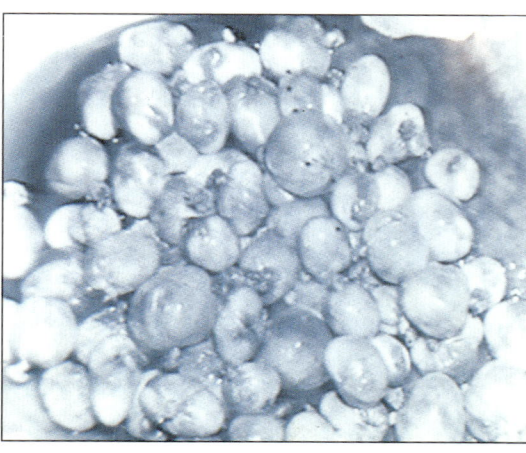

ILLEGAL TRAFFIC

The drug barons try to beat the Customs, especially when they have large loads to smuggle. They often use small boats and planes for their cargos.

Cocaine is loaded onto light aircraft which take off from small airstrips hidden in the jungle. Sometimes the drug is flown directly to the United States in secret. The aircraft land at night in deserted areas. Other shipments are taken to remote islands and transferred to small motor boats. These put the cocaine ashore at secret locations along the coast. Some cocaine is sent directly to Europe hidden in shipments of ordinary cargo. Some is exported through a chain of countries to avoid suspicion.

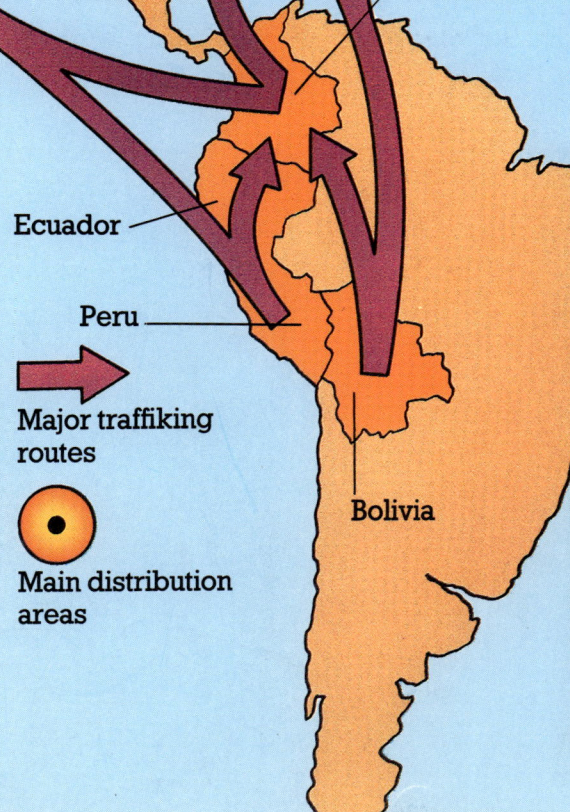

Large shipments of cocaine are worth a small fortune. Forty pounds might fetch $11 million, but the risks are very great. Many aircraft crash at night or trying to land on roads or makeshift airfields. Boat crews get caught and end up in jail.

14 WHY PEOPLE USE THEM

Both of these drugs give bursts of pleasure, but that is not simply why people take them. Cocaine is very expensive. Some people take it because they want to show how wealthy they are. Others try cocaine because they think it makes them appear glamorous or fashionable. If they continue using the drug, they find out that it is not just a plaything. Crack does not have a "jet set" image like cocaine. People take crack for three main reasons. First, it is cheaper to buy in small quantities. Second, crack is easier to take because it can be smoked. Third, crack gives a very powerful "high" which people soon develop a craving for. Drug dealers often give away free samples of crack because they know that people can become addicted after smoking it only a few times.

BUYING DREAMS

People who live in neglected inner city areas are often tempted to use drugs. Crack and cocaine offer a short period of "escape" from the misery of poverty and over-crowded housing. Under the influence of drugs, people can ignore the sadness around them. But after the drugs wear off they feel worse. The problems are still there and they want to escape more than ever. So they smoke more crack, and things get worse every time.

A STATUS SYMBOL

Because cocaine is an expensive drug, people think that it means money and success. It has become popular with young well-paid executives and "yuppies." Some like to show off their wealth by taking cocaine. But the drug can take over the most successful life. Many people have become addicted and lost everything they worked so hard for – their well-paid jobs, their fast cars and their luxury houses.

ROCK & ROLL MADNESS

People who live in neglected inner city areas are often tempted to use drugs. Crack and cocaine offer a short period because the drug gives a short feeling of confidence and energy. Rock musicians work very hard and get extremely tired. As a result, cocaine is a great temptation for them. But many have died because of mistakes with drugs.

16 WHAT IS THE EFFECT?

Crack and cocaine are "stimulants." People who drink coffee or tea are taking a mild stimulant called caffeine to perk them up. But when someone takes cocaine, they get a bigger feeling of well-being after a few minutes. This lasts for about a quarter of an hour. Some people call it the "rush" or "high." With crack, the "high" is felt right away, but the excitement fades after only five minutes. Then the user "comes down" with a bump and will often feel very depressed. Crack users tend to think only about their next smoke of the drug. Both cocaine and crack have dangerous effects on the mind and body. They make the user think he or she depends on them to be happy. Under their influence, the heart races and the blood pressure rises. Both drugs end up making the user feel sad.

WHAT HAPPENS?

Crack is usually smoked in a pipe or rolled into a cigarette. When the smoke is inhaled (1), it is drawn deep into the lungs (2). When the smoke is held in the lungs the drug is rapidly absorbed into the bloodstream (3) and then carried to the brain. There it has an immediate effect (4). It makes the heart beat faster and this causes a feeling of excitement. Crack works very quickly indeed, usually within seconds of the first puff. The "high" is very intense, because smoking crack delivers a large dose of the drug into the bloodstream. This "high" never lasts more than a few minutes.

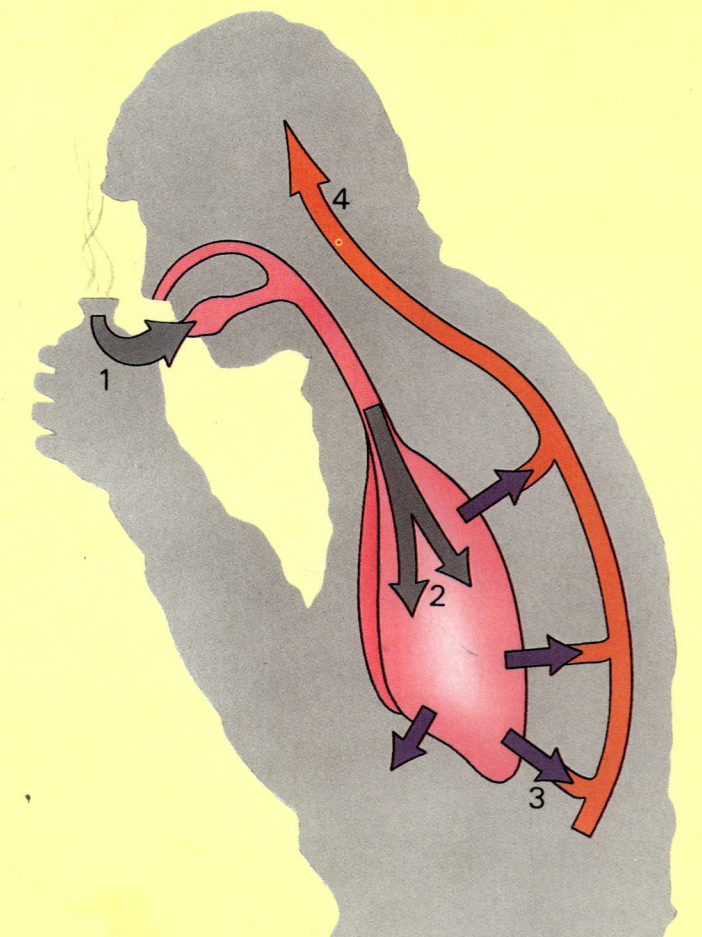

SMOKING CRACK

Crack is either mixed with tobacco and smoked like a cigarette, or burned on tin foil. Most users prefer to take it through a water pipe. The crack pipe has a bulge in its stem where smoke can linger, which means none is wasted. Crack users are so hungry for the drug that they use every bit of it.

TAKING COCAINE

Cocaine is usually arranged in lines on a smooth surface such as a mirror and sniffed, or "snorted," into the nostrils through a thin tube. The cocaine is absorbed by the delicate membranes inside the nose, and then into the user's bloodstream. Cocaine acts more slowly than crack, and the effects last a little bit longer. Frequent users often develop problems with their noses. Cocaine can also be dissolved in water and injected directly into the bloodstream. This is extremely dangerous because there is often no way you can tell how strong the dose is. People have died of an "overdose" as a result.

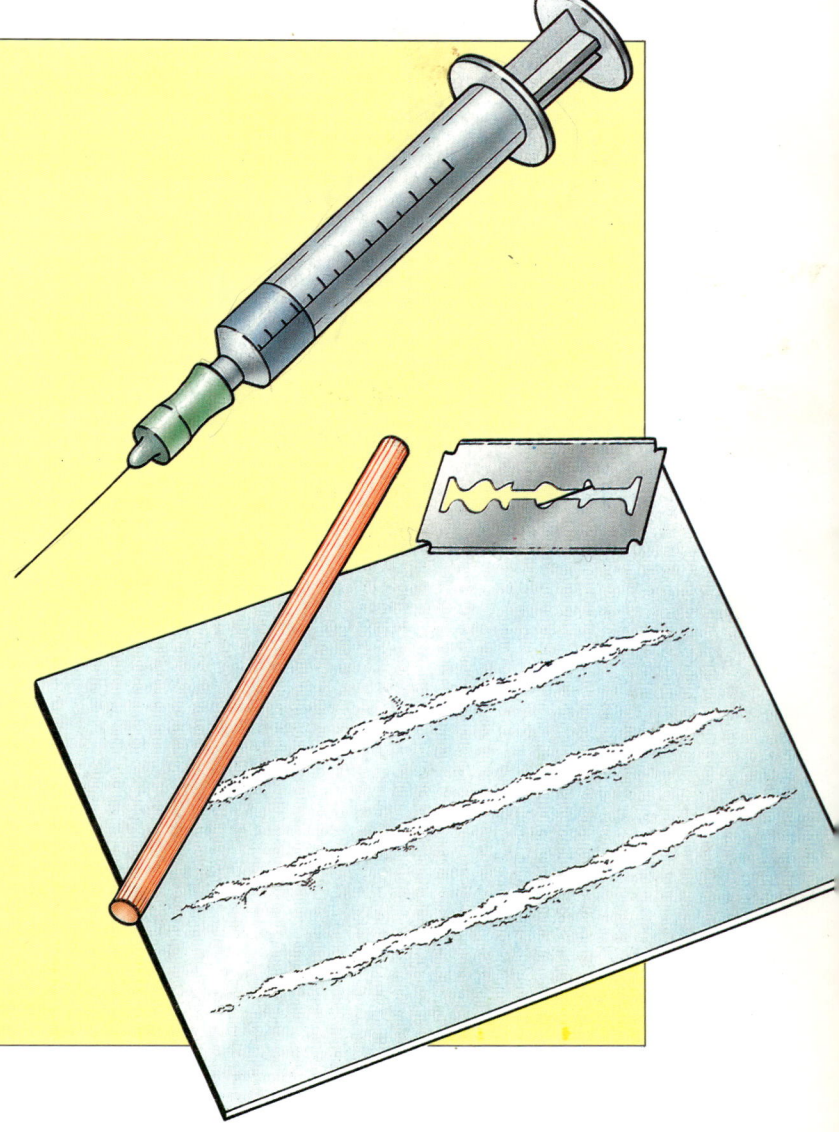

18 WHAT ABOUT THE AFTER-EFFECTS?

After the "high," a user does not return to a normal state. The after-effects of cocaine and crack produce an equally strong "low" or depression. The only thing that seems important then is getting hold of more of the drug. This can be the beginning of addiction. People who try to get away from the "low" by using more drugs can quickly become taken over by their craving for the drug. Some people snort so much cocaine that their noses are eaten away inside. They can stick a finger through one nostril and have it come out of the other. By this time they have constantly runny noses. Injecting cocaine too often can harden the veins so that needles cannot penetrate them. This could lead to serious problems if the user needs medical treatment.

BRAIN
Apart from personality changes, cocaine and crack can cause fatal brain seizures. The latest research shows that the drugs can also permanently affect the delicate chemistry that makes the brain work.

THE DANGERS
Besides the threat of addiction, crack and cocaine can damage your health and threaten your life. Nerve signals can become completely scrambled. When this occurs, the brain can send messages to the body that command it to stop breathing. Increased heart rate and blood pressure puts extra strain on the body. Sometimes this causes chest pain, in other cases the heart stops beating altogether. The use of crack and cocaine has been linked to sudden heart attacks in young people. Some of the victims were trying them for the first time. These drugs can also affect other organs, like the lungs and kidneys.

SKIN
Users get a sensation of "crawling insects" all over their body.

LUNGS
Small fragments of crack and cocaine can be inhaled. These can cause serious damage inside the lungs.

HEART
The heart is put under a huge strain by these drugs. They can cause heart attacks even in young, very fit people.

APPETITE
Crack and cocaine use reduces appetite. Users often stop eating, lose weight, and become very weak. They do not get the vitamins necessary to live a healthy life or to cope with illness.

20 THE BOTTOM LINE

The long-term effects of taking crack or cocaine are very serious. After the bursts of pleasure, pain and problems always follow. Snorting cocaine can cause permanent damage to the delicate lining of the nose. Smoking crack can cause personality changes, as well as problems with blood pressure, the throat and lungs. Worst of all, these drugs damage the muscles of the heart. This is very serious and it can lead to heart attacks. But even if the body is strong there are other dangers.

The latest research into crack and cocaine has produced some alarming information. The drugs seem to affect the area of the brain that feels pleasure – the "reward center." Crack and cocaine overload this part of the brain. The delicate chemistry of the brain can be permanently changed. The long-term effect is that users think they can only feel pleasure while under the influence of the drugs. Without crack or cocaine they become miserable, and everyday life becomes impossible.

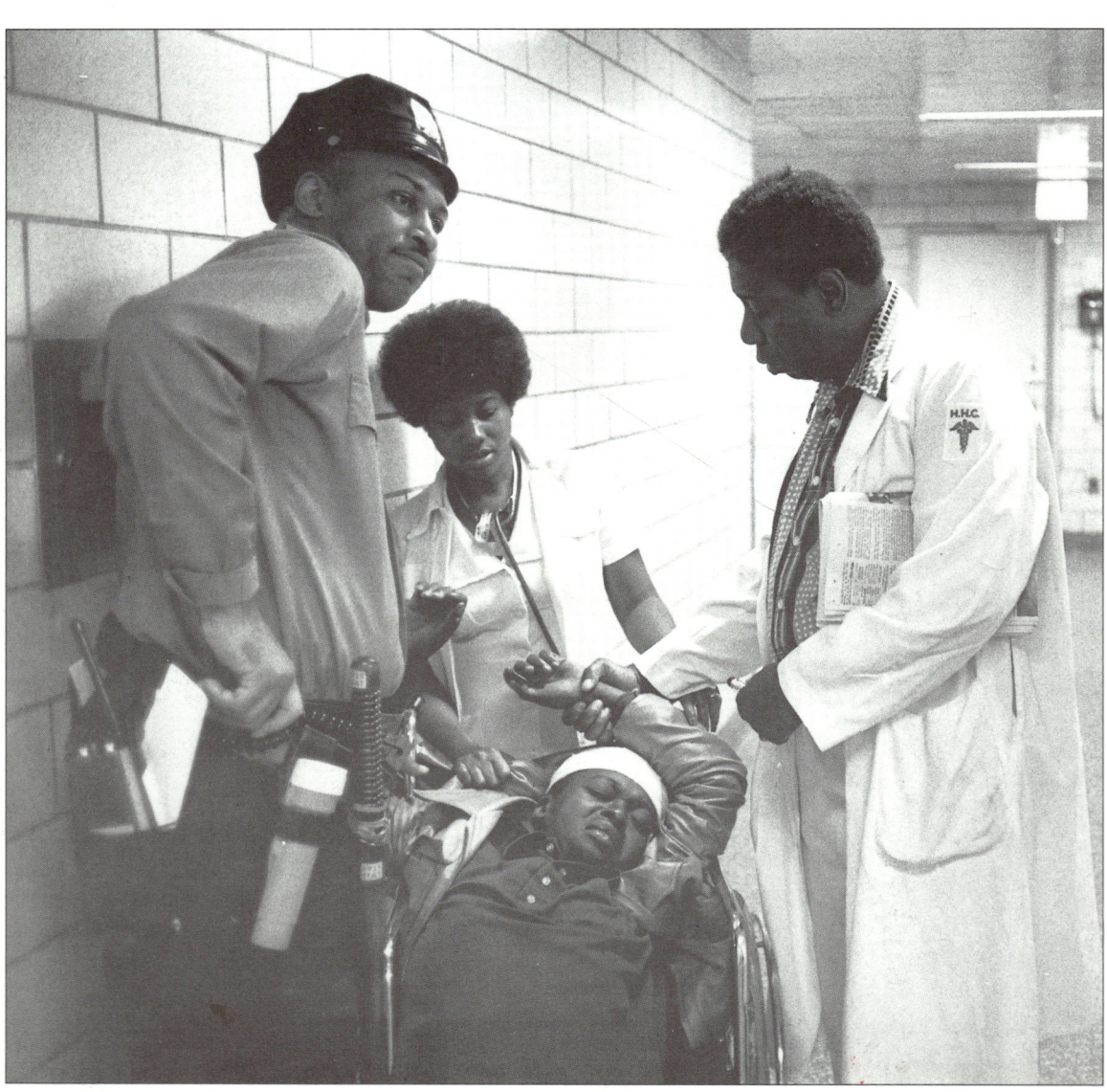

CRIME, DEATH AND DESTRUCTION

When crack dependence spreads in a city the results are terrifying. In 1988 New York hospitals reported that the number of people admitted because of crack rose by 86 percent. In the same year in the United States, one person every hour was arrested for a crack-related offence. These are all people driven to crime by this dangerous drug. Fame and fortune are no defence against cocaine. John Belushi was one of America's most popular comedians. He was fond of taking cocaine along with other drugs like alcohol. As a result, he died of a massive overdose in 1982. Len Bias was a star basketball player who liked taking cocaine. He was only 22 years old when he died of a heart attack because of his habit. The actor Stacey Keach spent six months in a British jail because he was caught by Customs with cocaine in his suitcase. It nearly ruined his career. He has since kicked the habit and joined many others in the fight against crack and cocaine. He said that even being in jail was better than being a prisoner of cocaine.

Stacy Keach

John Belushi

Len Bias

ADDICTION

When a person takes crack or cocaine, they feel excited and confident at first. The drugs allow them to escape from their everyday lives. Afterwards, the user can experience a deep depression. This encourages some people to take more of the drug. Soon, he or she is convinced that it is not possible to be happy, or even live, without them. This is the start of drug dependence or "addiction." It is not the user's body that depends on the drug. He or she would not die if they stopped taking the drugs. The dependence is all in the mind. Not everybody who tries cocaine becomes an addict, but they all run that risk. On the other hand, a person can become addicted to crack after the first few smokes. Crack is far more addictive than cocaine.

TRAPPED BY A HABIT

Cocaine and crack are very expensive, and so users often try to pay for their habit by selling the drugs to their friends and acquaintances. This sort of small scale drugdealing leads many people into serious trouble. It isn't simply that it is a crime. Drug dealers are often violently jealous of anyone who competes with them. Beatings and murders are everyday occurrences in their world. Once you are in with them it is almost impossible to get free. Dealers tend to take more of the drugs because they are around so much. This can increase their addiction and debts. So they have to sell more and more drugs. Crack and cocaine dealing is now a big business. Some dealers would not hesitate to kill a 14-year-old competitor.

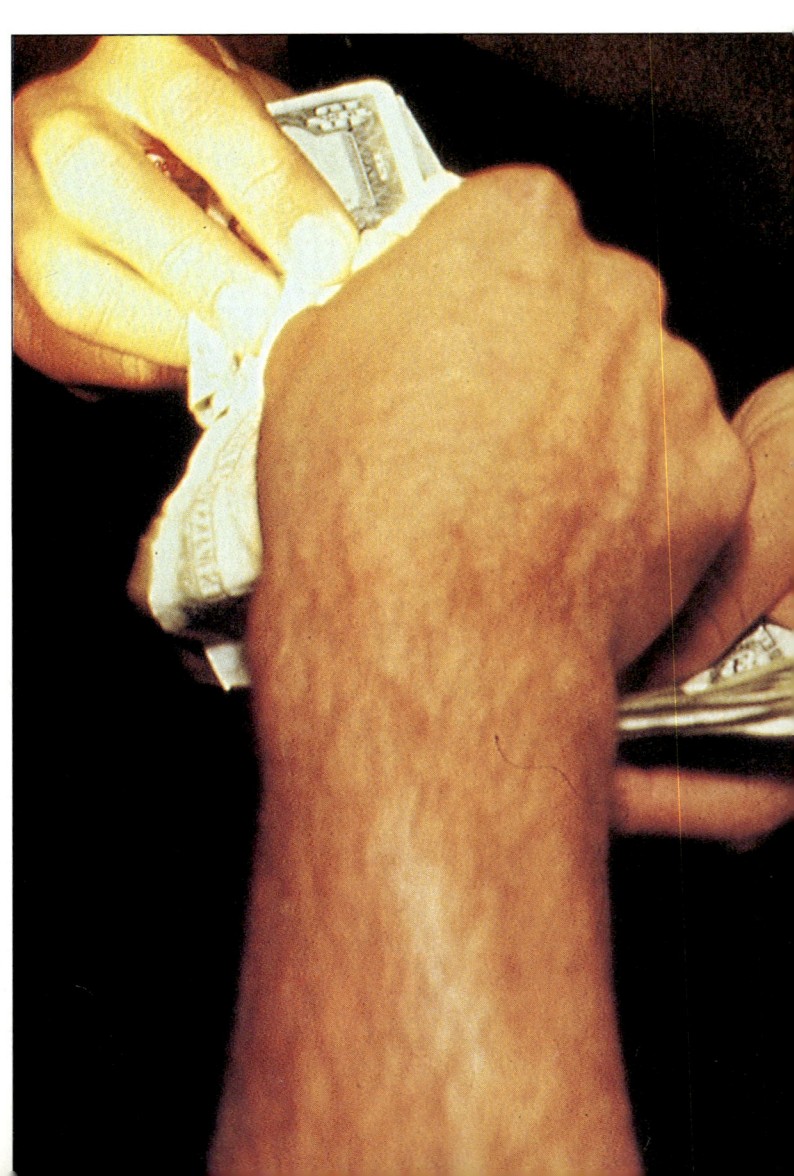

DRUG DENS

In the United States, crack dealers have set up special "crack houses" in which addicts can hide from the police. Crack houses have steel doors and bars on the windows. They are usually dark and damp rooms in condemned buildings about to be torn down. Addicts can go there to smoke crack until they run out of money. They don't seem to mind how run-down and dangerous the dens are. If the police find the house, it takes them a long time to break in. In the meantime, all the evidence can be destroyed.

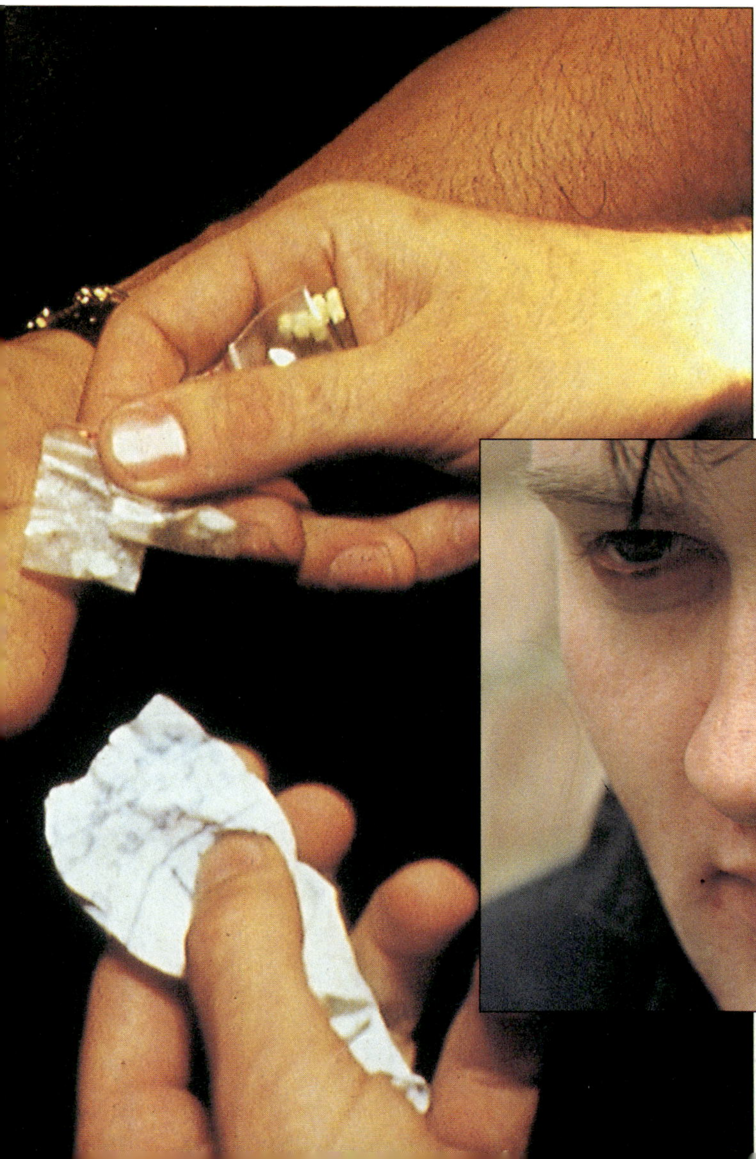

WITHDRAWAL

The only way to break a drug addiction is to stop taking the drug. Addicts think they cannot cope with life if they stop taking crack or cocaine. There are some side-effects, such as feeling depressed, irritable or disorientated. But these are only psychological and soon pass.

SOCIETY SUFFERS

Drug users often think that they are hurting no one but themselves. This is never true. Their activities affect everyone in society. Most addicts have to turn to crime to pay for their drugs. They start by stealing from family and friends. Addicts then turn to violent crime such as mugging strangers in the street in order to pay for their habit. Every crime has its victim, although crack addicts seldom stop to think about what they are doing. It is not only young people who can get hooked on drugs. Parents may also become addicts. When this happens, their children are neglected. Money that should be used to pay for their food goes to buy drugs. Without the guidance of their parents, young children can also become cocaine and crack dealers or addicts. This is one way in which the epidemic spreads.

THE TRUE PRICE OF CRACK

In New York, some young crack addicts have become prostitutes to get the drug. This has caused a terrifying epidemic of a disease called syphilis. Young women are having babies that are stillborn or handicapped because of the disease.

MURDERERS AND GUNMEN

In some parts of South America the violence of the drug barons has become part of daily life. In 1985 they massacred 40 farmers in Peru who would not break the law for them. But it is not just the poor who live in fear. The Colombian Minister of Justice tried to fight the drug barons, but was killed by their assassins in 1984. Judges and journalists have been threatened or murdered. Bribery and corruption, called "payola", sometimes rules more than the politicians, police or army do. This is just another way in which cocaine is ruining people's lives. Many of the drug barons can afford their own private armies of gunmen. They rule with either terror or rich rewards.

THE END OF THE LINE

Crack and cocaine have led thousands of people into crime. The law court officials have little sympathy with any sort of drug-related crime. Under the influence of crack, mugging can easily become murder. Drug dealers threaten the health of society. They have helped the drug barons to spread an epidemic of crime. In response, society gets tough. In the United States, more than 5,000 drug dealers were jailed in 1987. The average sentence was more than five years each.

SOCIETY IS FIGHTING BACK

The use of crack and cocaine is a major problem in the United States and in Europe. Governments cooperate to stop drug smugglers, and they tell the police to work harder at tracking down the drug barons. But governments need the cooperation of ordinary people in order to protect us.

Anti-drug campaigns do help. Most are aimed at young people who are the most at risk. The international "Just Say No" campaign was supported by Nancy Reagan, wife of former United States President. Local campaigns, organized by parents, are also effective. The World Youth Against Drugs movement has members in 35 countries. In the United States, REACH (Responsible Adolescents Can Help) was started by a group of young people.

ARMIES INTO ACTION

The war against drugs is now being fought by soldiers. In countries such as Peru, Bolivia, Venezuela and Colombia, government troops have declared war on the people who are making and smuggling cocaine. In 1986 soldiers from the United States were invited into Bolivia, by its president, Victor Paz Estonoro. They destroyed cocaine crops, airfields and laboratories.

CUSTOMS CRACKDOWN

The Customs official's job is very difficult. X ray cameras and specially trained dogs are used to detect drugs concealed in luggage or cargo. However, the money given to Customs to fight the battle is never enough. The drug barons are rich and better-equipped. As a result their drugs are still getting through. As always, the drug barons exploit the weaknesses in society. If we want to stop them, we must simply never take drugs ourselves.

28 THE BATTLE IN OUR BACKYARD

Crack destroys the innocent as well as the guilty. In Washington D.C., a 65-year-old grandmother was killed by a stray bullet during a shoot-out between crack dealers. In Florida, a 15-year-old girl was stabbed during an argument over a stolen car. She had been smoking crack.

The most innocent victims are the babies born to women and girls who are crack users. These crack babies are often underweight because of the mother's poor eating habits. In addition, they are addicts from the moment of birth. Many crack babies do not cry and do not feed. Without special care they soon die. Fortunately, people like Mrs Clara Hale do care. At her New York clinic, "Mother" Hale has nursed hundreds of drug babies to health.

GROUP THERAPY

Saying that you will give up drugs is a first big step towards a normal life. Staying away from drugs is very difficult, especially if all your "friends" are still taking drugs. Some former addicts continue to feel a craving for several years. Addicts who are trying to give up need all the help they can get. Many doctors believe that group therapy with other former addicts is the best method. By talking honestly about themselves and facing up to their problems, addicts can find the inner strength to do without drugs. Therapy and counseling can last up to five years. Such treatment can be expensive, but it saves lives. It also helps build up people's confidence.

HOTLINES

In the United States, several organizations operate crack and cocaine hotlines. These are run by trained drug counselors 24 hours a day. Callers do not have to give their names, and can ask for information or advice. Both adults and young people are taking advantage of this free service.

THE LAW

Crack and cocaine are strictly illegal. In the United States, possession of even small amounts of these drugs is a serious offence. Drug dealing, even to friends, means an automatic jail sentence if you are caught. In the 1970s many people thought that cocaine was a "safe" drug. Some argued that it should be legalized for use by adults. We now know that cocaine is extremely dangerous. Crack is even worse. These drugs have ruined thousands of lives. Trying them for yourself cannot be worth the risk. The cocaine trade is growing rapidly. In 1983 the US authorities seized about 26,000 lbs of cocaine. In 1987 the total was about 140,000 lbs – a six-fold increase. In Britain, Customs seized 77 lbs during the whole of 1984. In the first three months of 1989, the total was 484 lbs!

The spread of crack is even more rapid. In June 1985, New York police had not made a single crack arrest. In the first ten months of 1988 they made more than 19,000 arrests. This startling increase has much to do with the addictiveness of the drug.

INFORMANT LINES

One of the most powerful weapons in the war against drugs is the use of informant lines. These are telephone numbers which anyone can call if they have information about drug dealers. Many police forces operate these confidential services. In some cases, rewards are offered in return for information. There is nothing wrong about informing on a drug dealer. A dangerous criminal may be removed from society and your telephone call may help to save young lives.

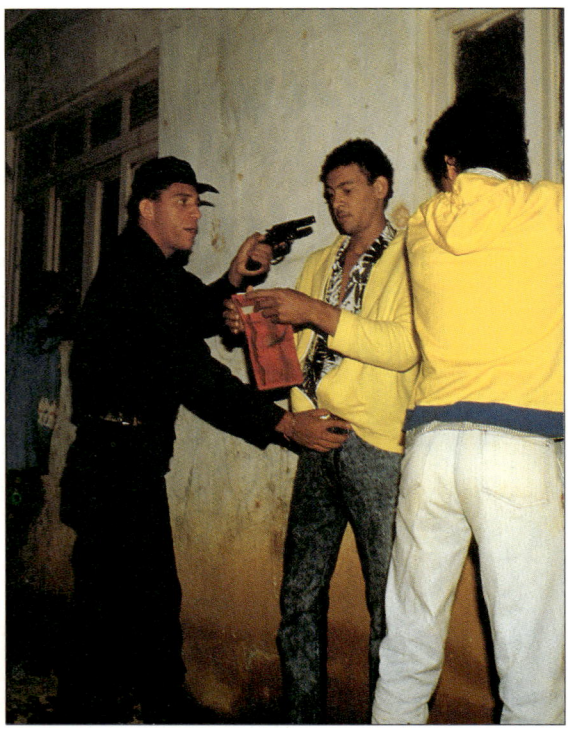

GLOSSARY

addict a person who is either physically or psychologically dependent on a drug.

coke slang name for cocaine.

crack a stimulant drug. The result of a chemical reaction between cocaine and baking soda.

drug baron a criminal boss who produces, buys, sells or controls the trade in drugs from behind the scenes.

high a temporary feeling of excitement or pleasure that follows the use of drugs.

low the sense of emptiness and depression which follows the use of drugs.

mule slang name for a small-time smuggler of cocaine.

prostitution exchanging sexual favors for money.

smuggling secretly importing anything into a country in order to avoid paying taxes or because the commodity is illegal.

snorting the slang term for sniffing cocaine.

stimulant a drug that causes mental excitement and makes the body's organs work faster than normal.

syphilis a deadly disease transmitted sexually.

SOURCES OF HELP

National Association on Drug Abuse Problems
355 Lexington Avenue
New York, NY 10017
(212) 986 1170
Offers family counseling and a drug prevention program.

Hale House for Infants
68 Edgecombe Avenue
New York, NY 10031
(212) 690 5623
Taking care of the children of drug addicts.

Freedom from Chemical Dependency
26 Cross Street
Needham, Mass. 02194
Conducts workshops in schools and "evaluation" meetings. After two meetings a counselor can refer the client to an appropriate treatment program.

INDEX

addiction 5, 6, 14, 15, 18, 19, 22-24, 29
agriculture 8, 9, 27
anti-drug campaigns 26-30

babies 24, 28
Belushi, John 21
Bias, Len 21
blood 16, 19
Bolivia 9, 27
brain 16, 19, 20

chewing coca 8, 10
coca paste 10, 11
coca plant 8-10
Colombia 9, 25, 27
cost of drugs 6, 13-15, 22
"Crackdown" 5
crack houses 23
crime 21, 22, 24, 25
Customs Officials 12, 13, 27, 30

dangers 19, 21, 24, 28
depression 16, 18, 22, 23, 29
disease 19, 20
drug barons 9, 12, 13, 25-27
drug counselors 29
drug dealers 10, 11, 14, 22, 23, 25, 28, 30
drug money 8-10, 12, 13, 22
drug trade 9, 10, 12, 13, 30

Estonoro, Victor Paz 27
Europe 5, 13, 26

farmers 9, 25

giving up drugs 23, 29

governments 26, 27
group therapy 29

Hale, Clara 28
health 18-20, 28
heart 16, 19, 20, 21, 22

impurities 10
informant lines 30

jail 21, 25, 30
"Just Say No" campaign 26

Keach, Stacey 21

law 7, 12, 21, 25, 30
Lehder, Carlos 9

Meza, General 9
"mules" 12

New York 13, 21, 24, 28, 30

overdoses 21, 22

Peru 9, 25, 27
police 12, 21, 23, 26, 30

smoking crack 6, 14, 16, 17, 20
smuggling 12, 13, 27
South America 8, 9, 12, 25
stimulants 16

tolerance 18

United States 5, 13, 21, 23, 25-30

World Youth Against Drugs 26